GUILTY
BYSTANDER

Lauren Shakely

RANDOM HOUSE 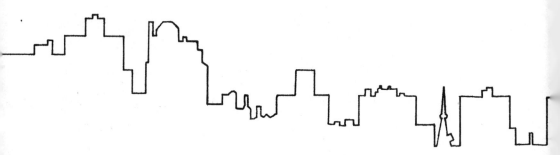 NEW YORK

GUILTY BYSTANDER

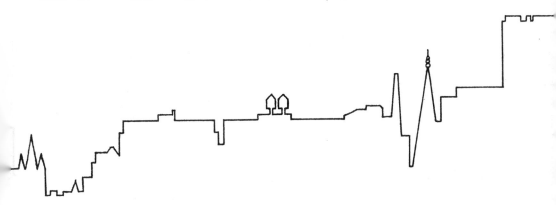

4/1978
Am. Lit.

Some of the poems in this book have previously appeared in the following
periodicals: *Caterpillar, Hanging Loose, Hecate, Painted
Bride Quarterly, Pequod,* and *Text.*

The author would like to thank the editors of Hanging Loose
Press for their support and assistance in preparing this book.

Library of Congress Cataloging in Publication Data

Shakely, Lauren, 1948-
    Guilty bystander.

    I. Title.
PS3569.H32G8   811'.5'4   77-13741
ISBN 0-394-42494-8
ISBN 0-394-73493-9 pbk.

Manufactured in the United States of America

9 8 7 6 5 4 3 2

FIRST EDITION

WINNER OF THE WALT WHITMAN AWARD FOR 1977

*Sponsored by The Academy of American Poets, the Walt Whitman Award
is given annually to the winner of an open competition among American
poets who have not yet published their first books of poetry. The 1977
award was supported by the Copernicus Society of America.
Judge for 1977: Diane Wakoski.*

Contents

GUILTY
BYSTANDER

Other Lives

my sister was in town last week
but she rescued herself
                    she receded into the Midwest
on an airplane she was afraid of
                    sinking back as easily
            as a stone into water
to spring in the suburbs—streets
                    full of cut grass
and oil dripping from parked cars.
for a moment
the side of her face
            flickered, a bright streak of mineral
flashed in the stone
but it was nothing
she hasn't forgotten
            bloody noses
and other horrors of our childhood
            games with the hands:
scissors cut paper covers stone crushes scissors
the vision this morning that woke me:
                    a pair
of open scissors shining on a rock
                    a stone poised above them
                    can't any of us be forgiven
for the choices we've made?

What They Call Me

Although in my family I'm known
as selfish and stubborn,
my name actually derives
from the crown of leaves
placed on the winning athlete's head
after the ancient games,
and from the only martyr
to crack a joke as he was roasted,
telling his persecutors to turn him over
and grill the other side,

and means "victory."

I'm sure
my mother never thought of that:
she named me for an ancestor,
either the one whose sword
still rests by the front door,
although no one knows
what side he was on,
or the one who invented frozen foods,
shipping pheasants to Delmonico's from Nebraska,
or the one who groveled in despair,
watching his children growing to the age
he thought he was
and his wife scrubbing
other women's laundry,
other women's floors

Letter to Yehudi Menuhin

music is not one of the important things in life
it isn't as important as war
or politics
or making love
it can't kill you
it can't keep you from starving
and in spite of their having paid $7.50 each to see you, all
of these doctors and husbands think you are crazy
because you play like you think music is just as important as money
you play like you're giving birth to a baby,
but I'm telling you for your own good
music is not important
and it won't help anybody
to die for it.

Don't get me wrong. I want nothing from you. I'm not your biggest fan,
and I was happy with my last row seat in the balcony, where I could hardly
see how fat you've grown.

But I want you to know, it was I who gave you the benefit of the doubt—a
broken wrist, I said to myself, arthritis, he's had a fight with his sister or has
eaten rotten fish for supper. Through the first movement and the second,
I worried and winced for you and prepared to clap the loudest—so when
everyone leaped and cheered, I was happy for you, if that was what you
wanted, but later I asked a friend, "How old *is* he, anyway?"

Actually, I don't care how old you are, but tonight you fumbled the way
I used to in my recitals—the jittery bow arm, the wood, not the hair, on
the strings. Since you were a Boy Wonder, you've probably never had this
problem. Let me explain it:

After the bow arm, it's the little finger of the left hand. Believe me, I know
how embarrassing—hitting it hard, say "E" on the A string, it always
happened to me—the little finger would lock on the note and wouldn't
let go. My other hand held the bow. I was helpless until the pianist finally
got up, lifted the little finger, and saved me.

So please, take it from me. When the bow arm goes, the hell with it. Let go
and play on with the left hand. Move your fingers fast and they'll applaud

just the same. Besides, you'll need an arm free when the trouble starts with the little finger. Hold the violin down at your side and conserve your energy for drawing blood across the stretched veins.

Admit it. You were lousy tonight. You think perhaps I'm just crazy in love, trying to get your attention, but after all, you're more like a father to me, and my own father wrote me today that I'd shown him how he had failed with his life.

Couldn't I do the same for you?

Advice

I didn't come to California to enjoy myself,
but to be depressed in a different landscape.
No one here appreciates how much better I feel,
since I've been diagnosed.
They grip their coffee cups
and demand change.

They don't want to hear about my father,
but these tense meals remind me of how he
used to bow his head at Christmas dinner
and carve so cleverly
he never saw the knife,
but what did he think he was doing:
Explain it to me, he'd say
Please, he'd say
Make me see
        What I see
is that to be needy doesn't mean
you lose your rights,
just your perspective,
or, as my mother observes about Californians,
they think dry grass is beautiful,
because they don't know trees.

My Father in a Foreign Country

After dinner, the coffee boy spoke to him.
He heard the sound, silver sliding on silver,
rose up blinking and dripping.

The ladies demanded satisfaction,
but my father said nothing:
the boy was so young,
the urn was so heavy,
the customs, as always,
so different from his own.

Family Portrait

When her dying grandmother
complained that there were no blue flowers,
my mother rattled off
bluebells, forget-me-nots, dutchman's breeches,
dispatching the old lady
with an encyclopedia of blue.

My mother
will not believe any mystery
she hasn't invented—
when she reads tea leaves
she never looks at the cup.

False History

I sleep fitfully
in my child's bed
under the pitched roof,
under the Babylonian stars.
Since I am alive it means
the wars are over.
We have eaten slumgullion,
a recipe my grandfather
brought home from the first war,
or Spam, which my father
learned in the second,
but it would be a lie to say
we are at peace.

On the porch my parents
hiss at their silhouettes.
My father tucks his hands
into his back pockets
and searches for the Big Dipper
in the wrong part of the sky.
He worries that this talk of money
will make me think we'll starve.
He's wrong.
I'm only convinced
they will abandon me and eat.

Against Life

From the first moment,
struggling along the dark canal,
a ring of muscles presses you
rhythmically on.
"Leave me alone," you want to scream.
Nevertheless you
break the surface,
a swimmer forced by biology
to take the air.

My friends at the beach
submerge into wave after wave,
yell to me alone on shore
about the joy of it.
But I hate water.
I know what it leads to.
And there is nothing in this life
that could compel me
to be born into it again.

The Accident

Once, nearly drowning,
I didn't call for help.
It was dusk; I was alone,
only my hair at the surface
spreading out and sucking in
like the tentacles of a jellyfish.

I was afraid I might be mistaken,
that the truth might be more elusive
than water in the throat.
Even a madman can often convince you
that his outbursts are jokes or lies.

With each breath I pulled
out of the vanishing air,
I realized that it's easier to drown
than to spend your life
trying to prove it could happen.

Those Sounds

Icicles melting at regular intervals
onto wet snow, birds surviving,
and the neighbor's German shepherd—
that once took my sister in his teeth
and carried her off—whimpering.

This white house contains a rug
endless as snow, but I choose the closet:
years later this fetid smell will put me back
to a sense of intense intimacy—
my arm wet where I have chewed it,
the pricks of color seen only
in total darkness.

A shaft of light splits a shoe.
I am so open I fall in love
with the scare it gives me.
My mother's voice through the crack
promises: "When you grow up,
you won't remember
any of this."

Stars

This is the first portrait I drew of myself
as an adult in the future: behind a flowerstall
I sell lilies with my hair unnaturally curled at the ends.
Over my head, the title: What I Want to Be.

They were all at her funeral when I decided
I could be where she was: I imagined myself
propelled into the night; I extinguished the stars,
drained off the darkness—then I tried and failed
to erase myself from this picture.

Her image also stuck.
My dreams were infected
with jars of cold cream, her brown teeth.
There was a lilac bush blooming at the side of the house.
The screen door banged;
she clutched two wads of my sweater
and shook me/ my teeth made music
my arms danced by themselves.
I saw stars.

A Bowl of Cherries

Ruthless baggage:
memory and symbol.
Like the ancient druids,
who were conned out of worshiping
trees as trees by St. Somebody,
we get itchy for metaphor
and that's that.

For example, my brother—
a prop from the past I hardly remember,
a chip of mosaic my mother
tucked in some corner
to teach himself to read or to
paste stamps in a leather album,
his fat legs motionless
as logs on the sofa—
has broken my privacy with a visit,
has come to represent
        summer heat;
             in Central Park
he inverts himself
on the blue sky,
shimmering trees—
he makes no sense:
of sunbathers on a hill he says,
"it looks like a battlefield,"
but he's innocent of decay—
he has only interpreted the image,
the way Christ seduced the druids
out of the woods.

Scorched Earth

Abutting every backyard was a field, used for nothing, intended for future developments. In summer, the grasses dried—long stems of wheatlike weeds to chew on, to bury yourself in, crying over some slight or punishment. The field caught fire periodically and housewives emerged, running from identical pastel bungalows, in bathrobes or Bermuda shorts, with pails and brooms, to drive it back. Sometimes, a fire engine was called, but usually the women handled it alone, their husbands at work, late afternoon, hair in pin curls, wash on the line.

Once, my mother grabbed the movie camera and caught me by the swingset, the fire smoldering behind me, dressed up in an old ostrich-feather evening gown from her days as a Southern debutante— with her beaded bag, high-heeled shoes, wearing her lipstick, her silver eyeshadow, her rouge—more decked out than I've ever been since. Unfortunately, the camera was loaded with indoor film, and the result was a blue movie: blue skin and eyes and grass. Blue women scurrying in the background, saving their tomatoes and rosebushes.

I smile shyly into the camera, waving with cocked wrist. A close-up of my blue face. I thought I could trick the grown-ups. Hammed up the act of childhood. Put in my time in my blue lips, blue-black hair. An imbecilic Southern belle, I was so fascinated with posing that later I couldn't identify the enemy that passed behind me, scorching out the possibilities.

St. Joan in California

The principle of her execution
is the one used today on forests:
backfires defeat fire.
It doesn't seem she complained much,
though, to imitate Christ, she must have carped
and died anyway.

Who'd have thought I'd curl back on faith.
As fear spreads it consumes all rational motives.
Taking her model, I march, with arms outstretched
into a grove of smoldering pines.

But in my secret version of her life,
she touches herself at the last moment
and cries out, listing what she might have done.
I must believe this: no one ever dies who can change.

How the French Take Off Their Clothes

Watching this movie—
the husband who loses control
of his wife, goes mad, kicks
her head in—I'm disturbed,
but not by the plot. It's the idea
of difference I can't stand.

I remember enough of childhood rules
to know that when you take off your clothes
the skirt goes first,
but in this movie, men and women
begin by snapping their shirts from their belts,
and this isn't even why
they feel guilty.

What I expected from life
was to become a fixed point, a pole
a man could tether himself to
circling, with his unappeasable hunger.
Yet I can't even stay to the end of this movie,
having to move.

The Wedding

The bride so attractive,
each tooth painted a different color
as is the custom,
limps from the penny in her shoe.
The maid of honor in pastel
is reproduced ten times;
the best man, in black, the same.

The priest, the bride, the groom, etc.,
take turns mumbling into the microphone.
The best man gives the ring to the altar boy.
The altar boy runs around the altar,
kneeling and crossing twice in transit,
hands the ring to the priest.
The priest gives the microphone to the best man.
The groom gives the ring to the bride,
mumbling into the microphone.

The priest pours wine and drinks it all himself,
washes the dishes, blesses the dishes,
puts the dishes in a gold vault
to keep the blessing fresh.
The priest blesses salad dressing
for the parents of the bride and groom.
The bride admires a statue
and presents her mother with a yellow rose.

The priest takes the bride's hand.
The groom leaps up and challenges the priest,
an error that will surely be forgotten
in the happy days ahead.

Manifest Destiny

As a child I accepted
that no man could be an island,
but I figured that any man
could be a peninsula,
any man could touch
at only one point of his choice

In Ohio, stepping onto a porch
overlooking the stockyards,
I could hear the train whistling
and hogs screaming
over melting snow,
spilled gasoline

Boston smells like this,
Princeton, Washington, and even Rome
smell like this,
and even in New York,
where I can't smell anything,
a man ties me down to the landscape.
When he clutches my waist in his sleep I dream
I'm the Siamese twin of a madman.

Lunatics

On the cover
she is tall, blond, cool,
the scientist in safari khakis
trailing a chimp through the jungle;
on the page
she is syrup:
"David [she names the ape]
looked up, our eyes met," etc.

Around me the subway walls
are spattered with names,
violent and tender
spirals and strokes—
names only. As in the beginning,
after the first man had separated,
in his mind, the animals,
he named them. Not even
David the ape
would have done such a thing.

How crazy you thought I was last night,
banging my head on the doorjamb.
You think I'd be saner
in a primitive career:
splitting railroad ties,
operating the spreader, the tractor,
or knitting you socks.
But can't self-awareness alone
redeem a madman?

If I thought origins were important
I'd be down on my knees in the jungle
kissing ape toes, telling stories to apes.

True love begins with the identification
of your own species,
and I wouldn't love anyone
who wasn't as crazy as I am.

The Monster Heart

I want my heart to rush after other hearts
like a taxi trying to make a light.
Think of it:
the monster heart
the heart that ate New York,
a heart that solves arguments between lovers
by offering to love them both
if they promise to keep quiet,
a heart that, when interviewed on TV,
answers politely,
"No thank you, I only eat other hearts,"
and never mentions me personally—
a heart anyone could love,
if he didn't already know
what was wrong with it

Concert in the Park

the trumpet stutters
the French horn drowns in his half-felt kiss
the music is so bad I can't ignore you
beside me on your haunches
pawing and whining for love

of all the things you're blind to
you especially can't see
my fatigue
with this hot night, this life
in which there is nothing to anticipate
but watching the worst in yourself
begin to bloom in someone else,

and your desperation
as real and as temporary
as a musician's floundering through a piece
he was sure he could play

For the Love of Anchovies

1

I love anchovies
the way I once loved you.
That's right: anchovies,
dark-skinned, bathed in oil,
curled lovingly around capers
or spread flat on the plate,
hands behind heads,
feet tucked,
ribs bristling—
I almost go down on my knees
at the thought.

The love of anchovies
is taking over my life.
I sneak into Italian groceries
to buy four or five cans at a time.
I'm unable to bypass Caesar salad
on any menu,
and my friends are worried.
I could forget rolling back the lid with the key,
the first glimpse, recognition,
everything—
but the taste.

2

The first time I ate anchovies
was in 1969.
The man I lived with—
the one you called "the lease,"
because it wasn't going to last—
ordered antipasto.
My first anchovy
slid bones first into my throat
and choked me. It's a mystery

how I came to love them
after that.

3

One night after eating anchovies
I dreamed of you.
You'll be glad to know
I wasn't in love this time.
I regarded you as I would
a familiar vegetable.
Your shirt was off;
your stomach hung pendulously
over your belt, like a yellow squash.

Let's face it: your neck
has begun to hold its crease;
your ears sprout whiskers. Naturally,
I'm afraid of the warning signs of death.
Why you didn't love me
is another story—this
is a tribute to new love,
anchovies I stroke tenderly with my fingernail,
whose odor I carry shyly
into my daily life.

In the Ladies' Room

you can read in the Bible
how just thinking about it
is as good as doing it

but I can't think—
a compact with a mirror snaps shut
on another woman's face

is it so strange
I should compare myself with God,
who denies me everything?

Wounds

Only in dreams can I carry it off:
at resort hotels on exotic islands
door-to-door salesmen
and other strangers
mysteriously plummet from balconies
and bleed to death in marble lobbies,
attended by perplexed and angry policemen,
who know that I'm the butcher
and who wonder
why I don't send the heads
of my faithless lovers
rolling down San Juan Avenue,
why I don't hang their heads like coconuts
from the palms around the square.

The Bartender's Back

I am the only customer in this bar.
The bartender has flirted with me,
he has taken my money,
and has turned his back to me,
shifting his bones under taut skin.
I want to caress the bartender's back,
but I catch my hand, disembodied, hovering
in the mirror, and arrest it.

Drunk in the ladies' room,
I lean over the sink and rail at myself,
pants bunched at my ankles.
Then the two of us accuse a third
of wandering off with the best and easiest life.
How can I sustain a single identity
long enough to satisfy desire?
At least when I test a razor against my cheek,
I can see it is unnecessary.

Living Among Reptiles

Love goes out with a hiss,
but he doesn't hear it
and I don't tell him.

I beat my wings in my sleep,
until he says he cannot bear the roar
or the scars afterwards.

He is the lizard who oozed in under the door,
and when he turns his spines to me,
I let him have it.

Giving Birth

In the dream you midwifed
while I waited on my back,
staring at the yellow bulb;

then it came all at once,
easy & slippery—
we watched it slide into the room
face up, a skinny kid
with fishy limbs and blank eyes,
and so much like us
we had to throw it out

Necrophilia in Nature

First thing I see in the park
is a male pigeon,
its feathers ruffed,
attempting to mate with another,
dead pigeon, sex unknown,
under a tree.

I wonder:
didn't he know or care?
Has he been perverted by the urban environment?
Has the population of female pigeons so declined
that males must make do?
Or was he an individual,
self-interested and striking out?
Finally,
why did I watch?

It must have been
a spontaneous scientific investigation,
an attempt to reduce guilt
by extending personal feelings
to common fact.
Here we have
the perfect relationship,
the corpse indifferent, immutable,
the lover illogical, unswayable.
Here we have
frozen mounds of grass,
a flutter of wings,
worms writhing in their invisible tunnels,
and hope for the future:
the possibility that sex and death
might have something in common
beyond my fear of them.

Ulterior Motivation

I am following a man,
not because I want to,
but because he's going where I want to go,
up tenth street, down Broadway, across eighth.
Maybe there's someone behind me doing the same.
Maybe the whole movement of the city
is based on mutual surveillance.
Maybe this is the function of cities:
those who must be watched
are assigned to each other.

Terrible Strangers

The woman tipped her hairdresser
and stepped into the light, where she was
doused with gasoline and set afire
by a total stranger. She turned
black as a cinder and screamed,
"But I didn't know him."

Really, who can bear the unexpected?
The old lady next door complains
the change in the weather
has rippled her feet into giant clamshells.
Also today, while I ate dinner,
the police ran stiff-armed down the street
aiming at a stranger; the gypsies
lounged on their front stoop, watching,
but immune to news
and new faces.

As for me,
I don't ask much:
to know the man who murders me,
to murder men I know.

Two Pieces of Fruit

1

I've become one of the madmen
who frightened me when I first came here.
I stare through walls.
I enjoy my own company.
Sometimes, on the street, I neglect to be fearful.
I am so ripe with pain,
even my friends hover around me,
expecting a tear in the skin.

2

Dry leaves slap against the window.
I think they are bats with faulty radar,
until I see they are yellow,
and purposeless,
and don't try again.
Outside the funeral parlor,
an old woman in a blue dress
tugs my arm.
"I'm next," she groans,
"I'm next, I'm next."
It's too late for her
robin's egg blue.
In this season of apples, pears,
I could be hanging on trees,
but I need my hands for other things
and won't trust my neck.

Guilt and Atonement Underground

Years ago I swore
I would never give a beggar a penny
unless I could pay all beggars.
Now I tell myself either,
"This one's a phony,"
or, "He can beat my ankles blue with that white cane,
I'm sure he must have put out his own eyes
with his own hands."

But I confess I'm a sucker for the half-a-man on wheels.
When he rolls down the aisle
glued to his little platform below the belly button,
his head at knee level,
and using his knuckles like a gorilla to propel himself,
I nearly lean over and whisper,
"Half-a-man, where's the other half of you?"
Shot off in battle?
gangrene?
crunched off in some machine
making shirts for us?
or was the half you're missing
burned off by drugs before you were born?

I can imagine how in hospitals
they send off amputated limbs with the garbage,
but a whole half-a-man—
is it buried in a half-coffin on Long Island
under the inscription, "Here lies half-a-man
waiting for his other half"?
Half-a-man, how do you live, excrete, climb stairs,
what are the secrets of your life?
I want to feed you,
sleep with you,
give you a college education—

it is my hand reaching over,
plinking the quarter in your cup.

Long ago I gave up giving to beggars,
but I suppose that some of the coins
I drop on the subway
must fall
into the wrong hands.

Sculpture Garden

The tiny mayor
precedes his retinue into the light
where they freeze
to have their pictures taken.
Then a man and a woman
model clothes beneath
the statue of Balzac.
They're cold.
After all, it's February,
and the costumes are meant for spring.
The man smiles at me.
The woman blows soft kisses in my direction,
but when the camera ignores them,
they ignore me.
What do I care?
I am the audience
and my opinion is the one that counts.

Bitterness

On the bus I consider
the ways to die in the spring—
Could eating olives from trees in Mallorca
kill you? Olives must be cured,
and almonds, too, I believe. Yet so far
we have only flowers and it's fruit
that is murderous.

On the bus I look out the window
for a passionate man, preferably
one who would sigh and work as hard
as salmon do, struggling upstream,
but all I see are vagrants on park benches,
men and women, opening and closing
their hands.

On the Bus

A stranger beside me
opens her book and we read:
       Chapter VII
       You are invisible
       No one has ever seen you
Across the aisle a woman
explains to her friend,
       Pisces aren't creative
       they just like to be around it

These women sure have got
my number,
but how are they to know
I'm boiling over
I choke myself awake
in bed at night:
I'm afraid I'm becoming
a woman I hate, or
I don't like to think I'm still here
when no one can see me.

To the Kidnapped Whisky Heir

Lying back in the dentist's chair on Monday I overhear another patient claim she's in love with your picture in the paper. The receptionist says it's morbid to want a guy who's just been snatched, but the woman says she'll wait, and I think: it's no stranger than any story about love, and not just in history.

The next day they report you're buried underground with only enough water and air for ten days. But this is bluff. Lack of one or the other would do it.

Saturday on the bus I stare at the park. On one block, hundreds of upturned faces. Are they praying for rain? No, they're looking at your father's window, waiting for you to come home. The rest of Fifth Avenue is clogged with linked couples, but compared to your predicament, the idea of pairs seems silly.

Your father pays them off on Sunday. The police break down a door. The kidnapper says, "Hey, what's going on here?" You say, "Thanks, Dad, thanks for everything." But don't you hate your father really? For his money, for the way he pushes you around. Do you like the taste of whisky?

Last night a fellow in a bar said I shouldn't write about people I don't know. Shall we meet, then, and start a seminar called "Solitude?" I could discuss what I imagined you were doing in the tomb you were never in, and you could introduce me to reality: dollars, deceit and the trap of introspection.

Mortality

When they close the bar,
we continue drinking in the dark.
One man says "my father's dead,"
and we all drink to dead fathers.
Another claims that his is still alive,
and I blurt out, remembering a play or a friend's advice,
"you must kill him then."

But it is my mother
whom I murder in my sleep.
I withdraw the blade
and wipe it clean.
Only when I see the sheriff
coming over the hill for me do I think:
death is going to change my life.

Alchemy

A woman dropped her glove
in midwinter, in my lap,
and fell across me on the subway;
on my scalp the place she touched
turned cold, the cold spread.
A black hole grew in my vision,
in her face.

        In my dream,
scraping a circle of carbon
from the hearth I found
a hoard of yellow, yellow gold;
sifting the coins saw that the face
hammered on each was my face,
and on the reverse,
where the mint, the government,
or the date should be, the words:
        To Be Changed.

Matchbooks

If I had any initiative
I could have my choice of careers,
which offer themselves
between my shoes
on the subway floor.
To think that in two years
I could be something as useful
as a civil engineer
or electrician
fills me with anxiety,
only partly relieved when my audience—
seven Puerto Rican women across the aisle—
remove themselves and their chatter at 59th Street,
leaving me with a young man and his suitcase
and the desire to know why his sideburns
dribble into his collar.

We are all absurd.
I have a friend who speaks of the present
in the past tense,
forcing into every situation,
its inevitable failure
and look at me:
my reflection in the subway window
throws out a strangely warm and attractive glance
of terror,
which I've seen before in other eyes
and which I think may be the only fire to huddle around
in urban life.

The Vampire's Kiss

a man holds a woman's foot
it's all right
he's a doctor
his hands are bloody
but she feels no pain
they say if a vampire falls in love with you
it is like this
you feel nothing until it's over
then, only loss

all the women on the subway this morning
had big breasts suspended in cotton slings—
undressed, they would make a popular kind of movie,
though some audiences might prefer
to see a doctor lick blood from a woman's foot,
raising it to his lips and working his tongue
without tenderness

Different Classes

In Girl Scouts, working for the knot badge,
I taught myself to make a noose—
a wasted talent.
Still wanting to learn—this time,
responsibility—I bought a fish tank
and managed to kill.
The iridescent carcass of the first fish
stretched out on the floor like dried bonito,
the major export of the Maldive Islands,
an atoll off the coast of Ceylon,
where a few men imagine
they are making a living.

All night I heard that bubbling empty tank
and dreamt of a life underwater.
I become something like a clam:
I do not think; I do not worry;
I do not dream; sometimes I move
slightly. If I had the human talent
of knowing what death is
I'd think this was it.

Practical Joke

I'm apprehensive when the others
clamber over the dunes, noisy,
their faces swollen with moonlight,
and circle around a box by the lifeguard's chair.
What do I know about happiness?
When someone lifts the heavy wooden lid and shrieks,
I soar on the note, convinced
what's inside is a dead calf,
its head broken to fit,
green maggots on the slippery flesh.

But it is only a thick rope
they uncoil and raise over their heads to dance with
through the rough black spittle
of Lake Michigan.

Breaking Faith

When Voltaire's buddies
called him back to Paris from the country,
you have to come, we need you,
he wrote back,
I'm tending my garden,
you tend yours.
No one blamed him for overlooking
that nothing much grows in cities—
a man can only extend his vision
so far, so long.

A woman standing in a restaurant told me
anyone can walk away from you
anytime, doors slamming, never call again,
even as a man clutched her by the arm
and led her off.

The corpse I saw on the sidewalk this morning
may have been a drunk,
but his pants were torn
and the flesh of his thigh
showed blue.
Still, I can't hate a man
for dying, or not dying
under my nose.

It means so much to me
to forgive everyone
everything.

About the Author

Lauren Shakely was born in Cleveland, Ohio, in 1948. She attended Denison University in Ohio, where she received a Bachelor of Arts degree in English, and the Bread Loaf Writers' Conference in Vermont, where she was a Scholar in 1970. Now an associate editor at the Metropolitan Museum of Art in New York, Ms. Shakely has translated Apollinaire's *Le Bestiaire, ou Cortège d'Orphée*, published by the museum in the fall of 1977.